THE HORRIBLY FUNNY JOKE BOOK

by Kay Woodward

Illustrated by Chris Fisher

SCHOLASTIC

Scholastic Children's Books,
Euston House, 24 Eversholt Street,
London NW1 1DB, UK
a division of Scholastic Ltd

London ~ New York ~ Toronto ~ Sydney ~ Auckland
Mexico City ~ New Delhi ~ Hong Kong

First published in the UK by Scholastic Ltd, 2006
This edition published 2008

ISBN 978 1407 11112 4

Printed and bound by CPI Bookmarque, Croydon

10 9 8 7 6 5 4 3 2 1

CONTENTS

What do you get if
you drop a piano
down a lift shaft?
A flat miner.

What's fluorescent,
sweet and helps
children to cross
the road?
A lollypop lady.

Which sport do
chefs like to play?
Bowls.

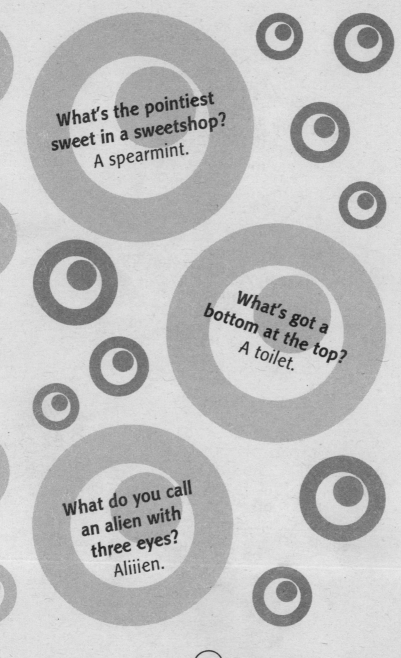

What's the pointiest
sweet in a sweetshop?
A spearmint.

What's got a
bottom at the top?
A toilet.

What do you call
an alien with
three eyes?
Aliiien.

What do snowmen sing at parties?
Freeze a jolly good fellow!

What happened when the boy went to buy a pair of camouflage trousers?
He couldn't find any!

Why did the computer go to the doctor's?
It had a nasty virus.

Why did the snooker player feel off colour?
He wasn't getting enough greens.

What do you say to a mountaineer who's sitting on top of Everest?
Hi!

Why did the satsuma go to the doctor's?
He wasn't peeling too well.

Did you hear about
the poetic alien?
He wrote uni-verse.

What do double
agents play when they
go on holiday?
I spy.

Did you hear about the
Christmas cake that was
whisked away by the
police without warning?
It was full of dangerous
currants.

Why did the clown throw cream pies at the audience?
It was jest for fun.

What happens when you throw eggs at a Dalek?
It's eggs-terminated!

What do marshal
arts experts eat
for dinner?
Karate chops.

How do you make
antifreeze?
Pinch her duvet.

How do you join
the boy scouts?
Rope them all
together.

Why was
Cinderella no
good at cricket?
She kept running
away from the ball.

Who dresses in red and white, carries a huge sack and has enormous pointy teeth?
Santa Jaws.

Did you hear about the juggler who could keep a broken TV, eggshells and a copy of yesterday's newspaper in the air at the same time? That's rubbish!

How do aliens lull an alien baby to sleep? They rocket.

Did you hear about the magical Y-fronts that couldn't do tricks? They were just pants.

Which type of gymnastics
are sheep best at?
The asymmetric baaaaaas.

What's a pig's favourite ballet?
Swine Lake.

Where do milkshakes come from?
Tap-dancing cows.

What do you give a poorly pig?
Oinkment.

What do you give a horse with a cold?
Cough stirrup.

How do sheep keep warm in winter?
With central bleating.

**What happens when
kittens catch colds?**
They get cat-arrh!

Did you hear about the mean old monster who turned into a pig?
He was a swine.

Did you hear the story about the miserable bear?
It was a Grimm furry tale.

The **100** Best Brussels Sprouts Recipes
by Pa P. Bottom

Trumpet Trousers
by Warren Oise

DIY Bubble Baths
by Wynne D. Bum

It Wasn't Me
by Scarlett Cheeks

It Stinks
by Will U. Stop

Mystery Smell
by Diddy Doowit

Down the Toilet
by Sue Ridge

Silent But Deadly
by Ike N. Smellum

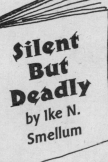

Addicted to Baked Beans
by F. R. T. Pants

What a Whiff
by Hugh Wozzit

What did the
cannibal say when he
saw Snow White and
the Seven Dwarfs?
Lunch!

What do hairy
monsters eat
for pudding?
Lice cream.

What flavour
squash did the
ogre like to slurp?
Lemon and slime.

How do monsters cook their food?
They terror-fry it.

**Which soap operas do
monsters love to watch?**
BeastEnders and
Coronation Screech.

**What do you say
to a monster with
a dribbly nose?**
Goo away!

What happens when you throw a warty, stinky monster in the Dead Sea?
It gets wet.

What steps should you take if an axe-wielding ogre gallops towards you?
Great big ones!

What do you get if you cross the Abominable Snowman with a vampire?
Frostbite.

What happens when an ogre with a big head sits in front of you at the pictures?
You miss most of the film.

Who won the ogres' beauty contest?
No one.

How does an ogre count to 23?
On his fingers.

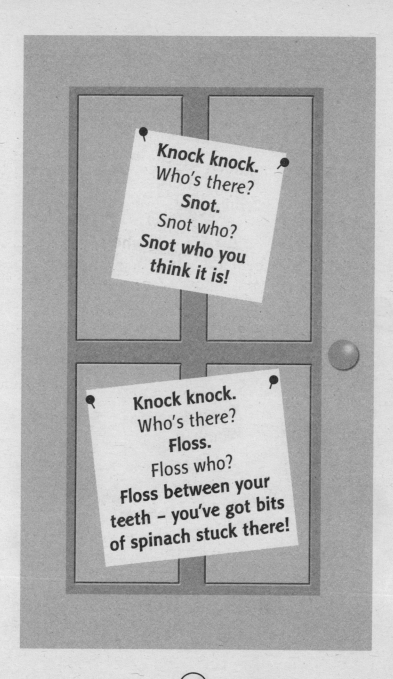

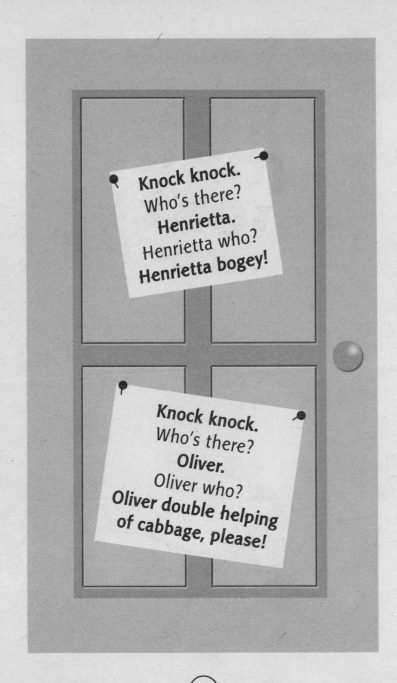

What do you call a
cockerel with a gag?
A cock-a-doodle-don't.

Did you hear
about the really
brave turkey?
It wasn't chicken.

Why did the comedian
laugh at his fried egg?
He thought it was a
really funny yolk.

Did you hear the
one about the
speedy boiled egg?
It couldn't be beaten.

What was the egg's favourite outfit?
A shellsuit.

Why did the chicken carry an umbrella?
The weather was fowl.

What's hairy and sneezes? A coconut with a cold.

When is a hot vegetable not a hot vegetable? When it's a chilli.

Why do golf players wear two jumpers? In case they get a hole in one.

Why was
Shakespeare buried in
Stratford-upon-Avon?
Because he
was dead.

What do you call
someone who sits in a
doctor's waiting room
for hours and hours?
Patient.

What kind of stories
do sailors' children
listen to at bedtime?
Ferry tales.

What was the maths teacher's favourite meal?
Pi.

What do karate experts catch in wintertime?
Kung-flu.

What do you call a man with a seagull on his head?
Cliff.

How do you make a sausage roll?
Push it down a hill.

What does a magician
keep up his sleeve?
His arm!

What's green and
hairy and goes up
and down?
A gooseberry in a lift.

When is it bad luck
if a black cat
crosses your path?
When you're
a mouse.

What's black
and white and
red all over?
A penguin with
a rash.

Which king invented fractions? Henry the 1/8.

What's big, red and eats rocks? A big, red rock-eater.

What noise do hedgehogs make when they kiss? Ouch!

What's black and white and very noisy?
A panda with a drumkit.

What's black and white and black and white and black and white?
A zebra stuck in a revolving door.

Why shouldn't you ice skate on a full stomach? Because it's easier to ice skate on an ice rink.

When is a car not a car? When it turns into a garage.

Did you hear about the girl who was tap dancing? She slipped and fell into the sink.

What do you call a boy with his head down the toilet?
Huey.

What's the stickiest type of tree?
Tree-cle.

What has four wheels and flies?
A bin lorry.

What lies on the ground, a thousand feet in the air?
A millipede.

If a greengrocer had seventeen Brussels sprouts in one hand and fifteen Brussels sprouts in the other, what would he have?
Big hands!

What do you call a girl with a frog in her hair?
Lily.

**Why did the chicken
cross the road?**
To get to the other side.

**Why did the gooey
chewing gum
cross the road?**
It was stuck to the
chicken's foot.

**Why did the squashed
tomato cross the road?**
Because it was trying to
ketchup with the chicken.

**Why did the dinosaur
cross the road?**
Because it was 65 million
years BC and chickens
didn't exist.

**Why wouldn't the skeleton
cross the road?**
He didn't have the guts.

**What do you call the snail
that crossed the road?**
Lucky.

**Why did the squirrel cross
the road?**
To show the other squirrel
that he had guts.

**Why did the chicken cross
the playground?**
To get to the other slide.

What happened when
the chicken ate a big
pile of sage, onion and
breadcrumbs?
It was stuffed.

What happens when
you take the yolk out
of an egg?
It's all white.

What's loud, sticky
and made of phlegm?
A cough sweet.

**Why did the monster leave a
dirty ring round the bath?**
It was just scum.

**Why shouldn't twenty seven-
year-olds pick their noses?**
Just think how many bogies
would be up twenty noses!

**What happened when the
bogey was flicked at a wall?**
It came to a sticky end.

**What did the man say
when he swallowed a
big, fat, juicy maggot?**
Delicious grub!

**Which part of the loaf
did the boy with scabby
knees choose?**
He picked the crust.

What do you call a snail
with a housing problem?
A slug.

Why shouldn't you have Great-
uncle Bernard for dinner?
He'd be far too chewy.

What do you call a cat
that's yellow and weeps?
Pus.

Slug: Why is there a girl sitting
on your back?
Snail: That's not just any old
girl – that's Michelle.

What colour do icky sticky monsters paint their bedrooms?
Slime green.

What's yellow, gloopy and very dangerous?
Shark-infested custard.

**What do you call a terribly
polite child who steps in
syrup?**
Gooey-Two-Shoes.

**What's green and
wobbly and has a trunk?**
A seasick tourist.

**What do you call someone who likes to
pick his nose under the bed?**
The bogeyman.

**Where do you find
giant bogeys?**
Up giants' noses.

**How did the snail keep its
shell so shiny?**
With snail varnish.

**Did you hear about the man
who used his intestines as a
bungee rope?**
He was gutsy.

**Why did the vegetarian
take an instant dislike
to the haggis?**
It was offal.

**What's worse
than finding a
worm in your
apple?**
Finding half a
worm in your
apple.

**What's green and red
and goes round and
round and round?**
A frog in a blender.

**Which scary creature clings to the
end of your finger and won't let go?**
The bogeyman.

**What's a flea's favourite
way to travel?**
Itch-hiking.

**What do you call a fairy who
is allergic to soap and water?**
Stinkerbell.

cindersmella

The Princess and the Pee

Snow Wart & the Severed Dwarfs

The Elves & the Spewmaker

Poos (or Pus) in Boots

**Which film do snot monsters watch
on television every Christmas?**
The Sound of Mucus.

**Which sculpture came last in the
snowman-building competition?**
The Abominable Snowman.

**What do you call a three-headed
monster with stinky cheese in all six
of his hairy ears?**
Anything you like – he can't hear you!

**What's green and
goes boingggg?**
An alien on a
bungee rope.

**What kind of monster
loves to dance?**
The boogieman.

**What did the girl say
when the monster
doctor asked to look
inside her mouth?**
Arrrrrgggghhhhh!

**What do you shout when the
Abominable Snowman surprises you?**
Not Yeti...!

**What's the best way to
speak to a monster?**
From a long way away!

**What did the monster say when he
accidentally sat on the packet of biscuits?**

Crumbs!

Where do zombies go on holiday?
The Deaditerranean.

What is the Loch Ness Monster's favourite takeaway meal?
Fish 'n' ships.

**What does a monster become
after it's a year old?**
Two years old.

**Why do dragons
sleep all day?**
So that they can fight
knights!

**What do monsters eat
for pudding?**
Eyes-cream.

**Why don't monsters eat
nuclear power stations?**
They give them atomic-ache.

What's the difference between a flesh-eating sea monster and a goldfish?
Try fitting a flesh-eating sea monster into a goldfish bowl.

How did the Hunchback of Notre Dame cure his sore throat?
He gargoyled.

What time is it when a monster sits on your bike?
Time to get a new bike.

What do you say when you meet a three-headed monster?
Hello hello hello!

What do monster mums do with cars, buses and trucks?
They make traffic jam.

What goes ha ha ha THUD?
A monster laughing his head off.

**Doctor, doctor, my
nose is running.**
No, it's snot.

**Doctor, doctor, my
nose is still running.**
Well, run after it, then!

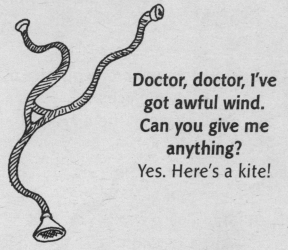

**Doctor, doctor, I've
got awful wind.
Can you give me
anything?**
Yes. Here's a kite!

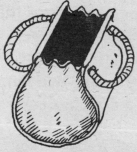

**Doctor, doctor,
I keep imagining
that I'm a leech.**
Go away, sucker!

Doctor, doctor, can you help me out?
Of course. The exit's just over there.

Doctor, doctor, I broke my arm in two places...
Well, don't go there again!

Doctor, doctor, I think I'm a bridge.
What's come over you?
Eight cars, two lorries and a double-decker bus.

Why did the haunted jelly fly round in a circle? He was doing a gloop-the-gloop.

What do you call a wizard with a furry face and a lightning-shaped scar? Hairy Potter.

What do you call a wizard with a furry face and a lightning-shaped scar who shouts 'boo'? Hairy Scary Potter.

What do you call a blood-sucking vampire who tells fantastic jokes?
Horribly funny.

What do you call a vampire who likes to relax in a bloodbath with a good book?
Well red.

Where do vampires keep their savings?
In a bloodbank.

Did you hear about the vampire who needed a drink?
He was bloodthirsty.

Why do vampires like thick books?
They like a story they can really get their teeth into.

Why are skeletons so lazy?
They're bone idle.

How do ghosts check that their paintings hang straight?
With a spirit level.

Why was there a road into the cemetery, but no road out of it?
It was a dead end.

How do ghost hunters keep in touch?
By eeeeeek-mail.

Why was the young ghost's birthday party so noisy?
His friends gave him the bumps in the night.

Did you hear about the really rotten spook?
He was a ghastly ghost.

How can you tell when a ghost is scared?
It goes as white as a sheet.

What do short-sighted ghosts wear?
Spooktacles.

Which part of a roast pork dinner do witches like best?
The crackling.

What happens when a ghost gets a fright?
He jumps into his skin.

Did you hear about the ghostly comedian?
He was dead funny.

Why was the bowl of soup so scary?
It was scream of tomato.

Why can't ghosts tell fibs?
Because you can see right through them.

What do you call a ghost with an upset stomach?
Spew-ky!

Which scary creature is always getting lost?
A where-wolf.

What's the scariest, squidgiest day of the year?
Marshmalloween.

Why did the alien land on the roof?
Someone left the landing light on.

How did Dracula
play tennis?
With a vampire bat.

What happened at the
cannibals' wedding?
They toasted the bride
and groom.

What did the hedgehog
have to say after being
trapped in the freezer?
It was a spine-chilling tale...

Why did the man's wig fly off his head at the end of the rollercoaster?

It had been a hair-raising ride.

What fruit do vampires like to munch?
Necktarines.

How can you tell when a vampire catches a cold?
Because of the coffin.

What happened when the ghouls bumped into each other at the Halloween Ball?
It was love at first fright.

Where do vampires spend their holidays?
On the Isle of Fright.

What would you find at a picnic on a haunted beach?
A sandwitch.

What do witches eat at teatime?
Spooketti.

Sticky, Crusty, Yellow Gunk
by E. R. Wax

It Came From Up Her Nose

by Luke Attit

Monsters Under the Bed
by R. Maffrayed

Wipe it Clean
by Lou Seat

The Good Bogey Guide
by Chris P. Wonz

Flicking Bogies
by Megan A. Mess

Catching Monsters

by Ivor Bignette

**Furry Hooters
and Schnozzles
of Germany
and Austria**
by Herr E. Nose

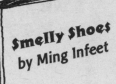

Smelly Shoes
by Ming Infeet

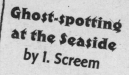

**Ghost-spotting
at the Seaside**
by I. Screem

**What happened when the sickly
cricketer bowled the ball?**
He couldn't help throwing up.

**What happened when
the gardener picked
his nose?**
He got green fingers.

**Which is the stinkiest
children's book
character?**
Winnie-the-Poo.

**Why did the mouldy
cheese disappear?**
It had gone off.

Which safari animal is really stinky?
A smellephant.

**Why did the comedy
mushroom go mouldy?**
Because he was a fun-gi.

What's the smelliest sport in the world?
Ping pong!

What did the scientist say when he discovered how to make a stink bomb?
Eww-reek-argh!

Why did the skunks start a fight?
Because they wanted to kick up a stink.

What do you call an exhausted man with a cow pat on his head?
Pooped.

What did the fisherman say to the vet?
Here's that sick squid I owe you.

**What's the smelliest
city in the world?**
Phew York!

**How many rotten eggs
do you need to stink out
a classroom?**
A phew!

**Why are bad eggs
dreadful comedians?**
They have such
rotten yolks.

Why was the sand wet?
Because the sea weed!

**How do you make a
teacher stew?**
Turn up late for school.

I have a warty
hooked nose,
flappy ears,
beady eyes, no
teeth and a
hairy chin.
What am I?
Ugly.

I have a warty hooked nose, flappy ears,
beady eyes, no teeth, a hairy chin and I'm
frozen to the spot. What am I?
Still ugly.

How do fish 'n' chip shops mistreat fish?
They batter them.

Why did the filthy burglar jump in the shower?
He wanted to make a clean getaway.

Did you hear about the clock tower that was filled with rancid cheese?
It ponged every hour.

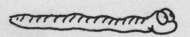